Power in Mistake

Bob Seeman

CyberCurb

Copyright © 2022, Bob Seeman

All rights reserved.

No part of this book may be reproduced, or stored in a retrieval system, or transmitted in any form or by any means, electronic, mechanical, photocopying, recording, or otherwise, without express written permission of the publisher.

ISBN: 9798371538826 (Hardcover)
ISBN: 9798371538406 (Paperback)

Cover design by: CyberCurb

Publisher: CyberCurb, Vancouver

Power in Mistake

About the Author

Bob Seeman is the Managing Partner of CyberCurb advising government and business on issues at the intersection of technology, law, and innovative business. He is a Director of the Cyber Future Foundation Canada, an international collaboration of industry, public agencies and academia to build a more trusted and secure internet. Bob is a Senior Advisor at Endeavor which identifies and industrializes game changing technology for the United States Government. He advises government and business internationally on technology, legal and business issues.

Bob has also published *On Trust, How Business Decisions Really Get Made, Quantum Quips,* and the foremost bitcoin-skeptic book, *The Coinmen.*

He is a California attorney, electrical engineer, and board director. Bob is a co-founder and former director of RIWI Corp., a public company that conducts data analytics. Previously, he was Head of Strategy for Microsoft Network in London, and a technical consultant to the European Commission.

Bob previously practiced administrative law with an international law firm. He holds a Bachelor of Applied Science (Elec. Eng.) with Honours from the University of Toronto, a Master of Business Administration from EDHEC, and a Juris Doctor (J.D.) from the University of British Columbia.

For Ahron, Geoff, Davey and Dori.

Table of Contents

Search for truth — 10
- Niels Bohr, 1885 – 1962 — 11
- Marshall McLuhan, 1911 – 1980 — 12
- Carl G. Jung, 1875 – 1961 — 14
- Martin Heidegger, 1889 – 1976 — 15
- Charles Darwin, 1809 – 1882 — 16
- Bertolt Brecht, 1898 – 1956 — 18
- Peter Drucker, 1909 – 2005 — 19
- R. Buckminster Fuller, 1895 – 1983 — 20
- Jules Verne, 1826 – 1905 — 21
- Franz Kafka, 1883 – 1924 — 22

Trying — 24
- Albert Einstein, 1879 – 1955 — 25
- Phillip B. Crosby, 1926 – 2001 — 26
- Euripides, 480 – 406 BCE — 27
- Bob Monkhouse, 1928 – 2003 — 28
- Marshall McLuhan, 1911 – 1980 — 29
- Theodore Roosevelt, 1858 – 1919 — 30
- Anonymous — 32

Learning — 34
- Plutarch, 46 – 120 — 35
- Earl Warren, 1891 – 1974 — 36
- Bill Gates — 38

– George Bernard Shaw, 1856 – 1950 … 39
– Ralph Nader … 40
– Zig Ziglar, 1926 – 2012 … 41
– Thomas J. Watson, 1854 – 1934 … 42
– Ovid, 43 BC–17 AD … 43
– Douglas Adams, 1952 – 2001 … 44
– Adam Osborne, 1937 – 2003 … 45
– Norton Juster, 1929 – 2021 … 46

Experience … 48
– Oscar Wilde, 1854 – 1900 … 49
– Denis Waitley … 50
– Franklin P. Jones, 1908 – 1980 … 52

Success … 54
– Soichiro Honda, 1906 – 1991 … 55
– Winston Churchill, 1874 – 1965 (attributed) … 56
– David Brinkley, 1920 – 2003 … 58
– Dale Carnegie, 1888 – 1955 … 59
– Conrad Hilton, 1887 – 1979 … 60
– Gisela Richter, 1882 – 1972 … 61
– Henry Ford, 1863 – 1947 … 62
– Thomas J. Watson, 1854 – 1934 … 64
– Bill Cosby … 65

Persistence in error … 66
– Marcus Tullius Cicero, 106 BCE – 43 BCE … 67
– Albert Einstein, 1879 – 1955 (attributed) … 68
– Anonymous … 69
– Anthony Robbins … 70

- Rita Mae Brown — 71
- Charles M. Schulz, 1922 – 2000 — 72

Excuses — 74
- Yogi Berra, 1925 – 2015 — 75
- André Malraux, 1901 – 1976 — 76
- John Kenneth Galbraith, 1908 – 2006 — 77
- Milton Berle, 1908 – 2002 — 78
- John C. Maxwell — 79

Coverups — 80
- Walter Cronkite, 1916 – 2009 — 81
- Bob Woodward — 82
- Anonymous — 83
- Henry Kissinger — 84

Forgiveness — 86
- Amit Kalantri — 87
- Voltaire, 1694 – 1778 — 88

Life lessons — 90
- Al Franken — 91
- Ernest Hemingway, 1899 – 1981 — 92
- Tallulah Bankhead, 1903 – 1968 — 93
- Mahatma Gandhi, 1869 – 1948 — 94
- Viktor Frankl, 1905 – 1997 — 95
- Stephen Leacock, 1869 – 1944 — 96
- Anonymous — 97
- Michael Ignatieff — 98
- Woody Allen — 99
- Anonymous — 100

– *Carroll O'Connor, 1924 – 2001*   101

– *Walter Annenberg, 1908 – 2002*   102

– *George Bernard Shaw, 1856 – 1950*   103

– *Napoleon Bonaparte, 1769 – 1821*   104

– *Oscar Wilde, 1854 – 1900*   106

– *Anonymous*   107

– *Jacques Plante, 1929 – 1986*   108

– *Doug Larson, 1926 – 2017*   109

Acknowledgments   **113**

Bob Seeman

Search for truth

"An expert is a man who has made all the mistakes that can be made, in a narrow field."

– Niels Bohr, 1885 – 1962

Bohr was a Danish physicist who made foundational contributions to understanding atomic structure and quantum theory. He was an acknowledged expert in his field, a no-mistake fact, confirmed by his Nobel Prize (Physics 1922). His definition of expertise is very apt; expertise can be measured not by one's number of achievements but by one's number of stumbles along the way.

> *"The specialist is one who never makes small mistakes while moving toward the grand fallacy."*
>
> – Marshall McLuhan, 1911 – 1980

McLuhan was a Canadian philosopher whose work is a cornerstone of media studies. He is known for coining the expression, "The medium is the message". He foresaw the internet but made a mistake by not appreciating the new medium's downsides. It is interesting to contrast his take on mistakes with that of Bohr. He doesn't think experts make mistakes along the way; he thinks they go straight to a final mistaken conclusion!

Power in Mistake

> **"Mistakes are, after all, the foundations of truth, and if a man does not know what a thing is, it is at least an increase in knowledge if he knows what it is not."**
>
> – Carl G. Jung, 1875 – 1961

Jung was a Swiss psychiatrist who, at first, formed a strong personal and professional association with Sigmund Freud. However, in his main work, *Psychology of the Unconscious*, he disagreed totally with Freud's thinking about the unconscious. The feud between Freudians and Jungians continues to this day. Both groups of followers would probably admit that each of their idols made some mistakes, but they would vehemently disagree about whose mistakes were worse.

"He who thinks great thoughts often makes great errors."

– Martin Heidegger, 1889 – 1976

Heidegger was a German philosopher well known for examining the question, "What makes human beings special?" What does "being" (German 'Dasein') mean? This question inspired Jerzy Kosinsky's 1970 novel and later film, *Being There*, starring Peter Sellers. Though extremely influential in philosophical thought, Heidegger made great errors, his worst being an initial fondness for the Nazi party.

> ## *"To kill an error is as good a service as, and sometimes even better than, the establishing of a new truth or fact."*
> – Charles Darwin, 1809 – 1882

Darwin was a British scientist who articulated one of the most important concepts in biology – the theory of natural selection. Natural selection is the process that drives evolution, or incremental change within species. He first published his theory in *On the Origin of Species* in 1859. Later, he proposed a theory called "pangenesis", an attempt to explain variation among individuals in a species. It was an error which the advancing field of genetics has discredited. Darwin's theory of evolution is a prime example of the power of a theory, one that has revolutionized biology, and yet is riddled with errors.

> *"The aim of science is not to open the door to infinite wisdom, but to set some limit on infinite error."*
>
> – Bertolt Brecht, 1898 – 1956

Bertolt Brecht was a prolific German writer (*Mother Courage and Her Children*), a citizen, at the end of his life, of East Germany. He supported the Communist government and did not condemn Communist purges. Eventually, however, he became wiser and realized his error. His point is well taken. Science doesn't lead to truth but it gradually erases untruths.

> **"The most serious mistakes are not being made as a result of wrong answers. The true dangerous thing is asking the wrong question."**
>
> – Peter Drucker, 1909 – 2005

Drucker was an Austrian-American management consultant whose core concept was "management by objectives". Many believe that this concept was a mistake since there's no proof that it works effectively. The concept is difficult to implement and, when trying to implement it, companies overemphasize control to the detriment of creativity. Nevertheless, it does seem true that asking the right questions gets you to where you want to go.

"Most of my advances were by mistake. You uncover what is when you get rid of what isn't."

– R. Buckminster Fuller, 1895 – 1983

Buckminster Fuller was an American architect, systems theorist, writer, designer, inventor, philosopher, and futurist best known for his geodesic dome. Fuller entered Harvard University in 1913 but was expelled after excessively socializing and not showing up for his midterm exams. He made a mistake but, given his amazing career, the expulsion may have been the best thing to happen to him.

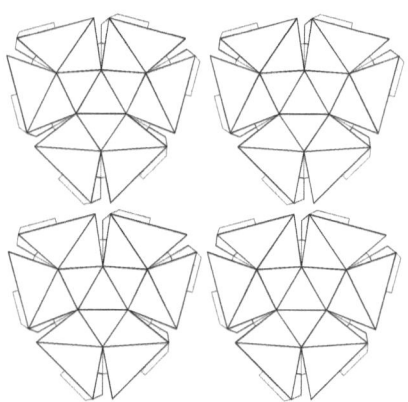

> *"Science, my lad, is made up of mistakes, but they are mistakes which it is useful to make, because they lead little by little to the truth."*
>
> – Jules Verne, 1826 – 1905

Since 1979, French science fiction writer, Jules Verne, has become the second most translated author in the world, coming between Agatha Christie and William Shakespeare. He predicted (*Twenty Thousand Leagues under the Seas, Around the World in Eighty Days, Journey to the Center of the Earth*) many things right, including submarines and landing on the moon. However, one big mistake was thinking that we would get to the center of the earth. This hasn't happened yet, but who knows?

> *" 'But I'm not guilty,' said K. 'There's been a mistake.' How is it even possible for someone to be guilty? We're all human beings here, one like the other. 'That is true' said the priest 'but that is how the guilty speak'."*
>
> – Franz Kafka, 1883 – 1924

Franz Kafka, now viewed as "the Dante of the 20th century" (W.H. Auden), achieved fame only after his death. "Kafkaesque" has become a common adjective that describes absurd anxiety-provoking situations akin to those Kafka wrote about in *The Metamorphosis*, *The Trial*, or *The Castle*. Mistakes are made not only by us personally but, even more, by the administrators of the bureaucracies we live in.

Power in Mistake

Bob Seeman

Trying

"Anyone who has never made a mistake has never tried anything new."

– Albert Einstein, 1879 – 1955

Einstein was one of the greatest and most influential physicists of all time. He is best known for developing the theory of relativity. However, when crafting his theory, Einstein needed a "fudge factor". Everyone at the time considered the universe to be static. To make his equations fit the known data, Einstein added a factor, which he named the cosmological constant, into his equations. When he later learned that the universe is not static, but expanding, he stated "Then away with the cosmological constant!" It was his biggest mistake. His quotation, however, is not mistaken.

"Making a wrong decision is understandable. Refusing to search continually for learning is not."

– Phillip B. Crosby, 1926 – 2001

Crosby was a businessman and author who contributed to management theory and quality management practices. He initiated the Zero Defects program at the Martin Company where, as the quality control manager of the Pershing missile program, he reduced overall rejection rate by 25%. He made a mistake calling his program "Zero Defects" but his quotation is right on the mark.

"He who does much makes the most mistakes."

– Euripides, 480 – 406 BCE

Euripides, along with Aeschylus and Sophocles, was one of the three ancient Greek tragedians whose plays (at least some of them) have survived (*Medea, Electra, Andromache, Orestes, The Trojan Women.*) Some ancient scholars attributed a total of ninety-five plays to Euripides. Some were mistakes and closed opening night, an inevitable outcome of productivity.

"When the inventor of the drawing board messed things up, what did he go back to?"

– Bob Monkhouse, 1928 – 2003

Bob Monkhouse was English comedian who messed up his first marriage. In his autobiography, he admitted to hundreds of sexual liaisons. After his divorce, he dated Diana Dors, about whose parties he later commented: "The awkward part about an orgy is that afterwards you're not too sure who to thank."

"Nobody ever made a grammatical error in a non-literate society."

– Marshall McLuhan, 1911 – 1980

McLuhan, identified in an earlier quotation, is wittily uttering a profound truth – the more we know, the more we realize how wrong we are.

"The only man who makes no mistakes is the man who never does anything."

– Theodore Roosevelt, 1858 – 1919

Roosevelt was the 26th American President (1901 – 1909). Daring to do mighty things was always Theodore Roosevelt's motto. Roosevelt's worst mistake, in a presidency otherwise relatively free of error, was his dishonorable discharge of an entire regiment of Black soldiers after an alleged riot in 1906. No Black soldier was allowed to testify despite convincing evidence that the riot was an invention of White racists. Roosevelt may have later realized his mistake but his pride got in the way of admitting it.

"Mistakes are proof you are trying."

– Anonymous

In 2012, Time magazine called Anonymous one of the "100 most influential people" in the world.

Power in Mistake

Bob Seeman

Learning

"To make no mistakes is not in the power of man; but from their errors and mistakes the wise and good learn wisdom for the future."

– Plutarch, 46 – 120

Plutarch was a Greek philosopher, historian, biographer, essayist, and priest at the Temple of Apollo in Delphi. Plutarch lived so long ago that that records of his mistakes have been lost in the mists of time. But he was wise. So he must have made many mistakes.

Ta fage inftruction fert de riche couronne
A Trajan, efleué par deffus tous humains.
Si les grands te portoient au cœur & dans leurs mains,
Vertu viuroit au lieu de Venus & Bellone

"If it is a mistake of the head and not the heart don't worry about it, that's the way we learn."

– Earl Warren, 1891 – 1974

Warren was the Chief Justice of the U.S. Supreme Court. He made a big mistake when, as Attorney General of California following the Japanese attack on Pearl Harbor, he became a driving force behind the internment of over one hundred thousand Japanese-Americans without leveling charges or allowing due process. Mistakes of the head, Warren seems to be saying, are easier to correct than mistakes of the heart.

> *"Your most unhappy customers are your greatest source of learning."*
>
> *"Success is a lousy teacher. It seduces smart people into thinking they can't lose."*
>
> – Bill Gates

Bill Gates is an American businessperson and philanthropist who founded Microsoft Corporation. Given all the error messages and frustration that Microsoft's products produce, Microsoft has accumulated more learning than any corporation that has ever existed.

> **"Success does not consist in never making mistakes but in never making the same one a second time."**
> – George Bernard Shaw, 1856 – 1950

Shaw was an Irish playwright (*Major Barbara, Man and Superman, Pygmalion*) and Nobel Laureate. He supported eugenics, a popular "science" prior to World War II. It turned out to be a pseudoscience and immoral to boot, championing the idea that man could breed better and better offspring and, thus, improve the species. Later, Shaw made an entirely different mistake – opposing vaccination. But he did not make the eugenics mistake twice. He did not support Hitler's eugenic ideas.

> ### *"Your best teacher is your last mistake."*
> – Ralph Nader

Nader is an American political activist, author, lecturer, and attorney noted for his involvement in consumer protection, environmentalism, and government reform causes. He made a career of pointing out other people's mistakes.

"Some of us learn from other people's mistakes and the rest of us have to be other people."

– Zig Ziglar, 1926 – 2012

Mr. Ziglar was an American self-help writer and motivational speaker known for his "Success Rallies" and "Born to Win" seminars. He wrote more than 25 self-help books and produced countless audiotapes on career advancement. One of his most popular lines: "Have you ever noticed that people who are the problem never realize it? They're in denial. They think denial is a river in Egypt!"

> *"Recently, I was asked if I was going to fire an employee who made a mistake that cost the company $600,000. No, I replied, I just spent $600,000 training him. Why would I want somebody to hire his experience?"*
>
> – Thomas J. Watson, 1854 – 1934

Watson was an American businessman who served as the chairman and CEO of IBM. He turned the company into a highly effective sales organization, based largely on punch card tabulating machines. Watson made one of the biggest ethical mistakes ever in business. In 1937, as President of the International Chamber of Commerce, Watson met Adolf Hitler. Watson's pursuit of profit led him to personally approve and spearhead IBM's strategic technological relationship with Nazi Germany. IBM provided the tabulating equipment (now in the Holocaust Museum) that Hitler used to round up Jews and other victims. IBM's punch cards served as a nineteenth-century bar code for human beings, identifying intended victims by name.

> ## "Who is allowed to make mistakes, makes fewer mistakes."
> – Ovid, 43 BC–17 AD

Ovid was a Roman poet who lived during the reign of Emperor Augustus. He was a contemporary of Virgil and Horace, who were older. This trio produced the canon of Latin poetry. Ovid was famous in his own lifetime. When criticized, as he often was, he responded (in Latin):

> *Gluttonous Envy, burst: my name's well known already; it will be more so, if only my feet travel the road they've started.*
>
> *But you're in too much of a hurry: if I live you'll be more than sorry: many poems, in fact, are forming in my mind.*

> *"A learning experience is one of those things that say, 'You know that thing you just did? Don't do that.'"*
>
> – Douglas Adams, 1952 – 2001

Douglas Adams was a British science fiction writer famous for the satirical book, *The Hitchhiker's Guide to the Galaxy,* which promises an "Answer to the Ultimate Question of Life, the Universe, and Everything." Spoiler alert: the answer, found in the book, is 42.

> ## *"The most valuable thing you can make is a mistake – you can't learn anything from being perfect."*
> – Adam Osborne, 1937 – 2003

Osborne was a British author, book and software publisher, and computer designer who founded several companies in the United States and elsewhere. He introduced the Osborne 1, the first commercially successful portable computer. It is said that in 1983, Osborne bragged about two advanced new computers his company was in the process of developing. The story is that those statements destroyed consumer demand for the Osborne 1, and the resulting inventory glut forced Osborne Computer to file for bankruptcy. This phenomenon, a pre-announcement of a new product causing a catastrophic collapse in the demand for older versions, became known as the Osborne effect. Osborne's name lives on due to his mistake.

> **"You often learn more by being wrong for the right reasons than you do by being right for the wrong reasons."**
>
> – Norton Juster, 1929 – 2021

Juster was an American academic, architect, and writer who was best known for his children's books, notably for *The Phantom Tollbooth* and *The Dot and the Line*. To combat boredom when he was in the military, he made up a fictitious newspaper called the "Naval News Service" as a scheme to get interviews with attractive women – something wrong for a good reason. He then made up the "Garibaldi Society" whose only raison d'être was to reject anyone who applied for membership. The only assets of the society were an impressive logo, application form, and rejection letter. Even Juster himself was not a member. Like Groucho Marx, he would never join a club that would have him as a member. Making fun of exclusive societies – his society was the ultimate in exclusivity – was doing the right thing for the right reason.

stakes are painful when they happen, but years later a ection of mistakes is what is called experience."

– Denis Waitley

is an American author (16 books) and tional speaker. Currently aged 89, he has ulated a lot of experience. The fruit of his ence is contained in another of his ions: "Expect the best, plan for the worst, prepared to be surprised.'"

Experience

"*Experience is [...]
men give to t[...]*"

– Oscar Wild[e]

Wilde was an Irish playw[right...]
remembered for his pla[y...]
Earnest and his novel *Th[e...]
is also remembered for [...]
"gross indecency" (hom[osexuality...]
advice of his close [...]
Marquess of Queensb[erry...]
Marquess publicly accu[sed...]
sodomy. To defend hi[m...]
responded by hiring pr[...]
that his accusation was [...]
the evidence that he [...]
result, it was Wilde wh[o...]
heed the advice of his m[...]

"Experience enables you to recognize a mistake when you make it again."

– Franklin P. Jones, 1908 – 1980

Jones was an American columnist. He also wrote, "A bargain is something you can't use at a price you can't resist." If true to his convictions, he recognized his mistake each time he fell for a bargain.

Power in Mistake

Bob Seeman

Success

"Success is 99% failure."
– Soichiro Honda, 1906 – 1991

Honda, dubbed "Japan's Ford," was an engineer, industrialist, and founder of Honda Motor Company. In 1937, he founded Tōkai Seiki that produced piston rings for Toyota. Tōkai Seiki was bombed and several plants were destroyed by earthquakes during the War. In 1944, Honda sold what remained of Tōkai Seiki to Toyota and, with the proceeds, founded the Honda Technical Research Institute to produce best-selling motorized bicycles and cars.

"Success is going from failure to failure with no loss of enthusiasm."

– Winston Churchill, 1874 – 1965
(attributed)

Winton Churchill needs no introduction, a great statesman with a knack for expressing himself in timeless words. He, nevertheless, had many failures. He failed twice to gain admission to the Royal Military Academy but succeeded on his third try. In 1908, having crossed the floor from Conservative to Labour, he lost his seat but ran for and won another. As Home Secretary in 1910, he failed to support women's suffrage. His greatest military failure was the Gallipoli campaign against the Turks in 1915 when he was First Lord of the Admiralty. After 8 months and a quarter million casualties, the campaign was abandoned. In 1922, he failed to retain his seat in parliament but succeeded in regaining another two years later. With respect to Indian independence, he called Ghandi "a seditious Middle Temple lawyer, now posing as a fakir." The derogatory meaning of fakir is: Someone who takes advantage of the gullible through religious fakery. Churchill initially supported Franco in Spain but later became critical. He supported Edward VIII's desire to marry Wallis Simpson and remain king. He considered the abdication "premature and probably quite unnecessary." Under Churchill's premiership during World War II, British troops lost many battles in Norway, France, Greece, Crete, and Singapore. Despite winning the war, Churchill lost the general election in 1945, but he again became Prime Minister in 1951.

> **"A successful man is one who can lay a firm foundation with the bricks others have thrown at him."**
>
> – David Brinkley, 1920 – 2003

Brinkley's was an American newscaster for NBC and ABC whose political opinions brought him a lot of criticism. His response was to expose the awkward, ungrammatical, badly spelled words of his critics' letters on air.

"The successful man will profit from his mistakes and try again in a different way."

– Dale Carnegie, 1888 – 1955

Carnegie was an American writer and lecturer, developer of "How to…" courses. He was the author of the best-selling self-improvement book, *How to Win Friends and Influence People*, that emphasized the claim that it is possible to change other people's behavior by changing one's behavior towards them.

> **"Success seems to be connected with action. Successful people keep moving. They make mistakes but they never quit."**
>
> – Conrad Hilton, 1887 – 1979

After serving in the New Mexico legislature and the US army, Conrad Hilton bought his first hotel in Texas at the height of the Texas oil boom. He went on to buy more hotels and to form the Hilton Hotels Corporation in 1946. Hilton was a cunning and innovative businessman, but made mistakes in his personal life.

"A series of failures may culminate in the best possible result."

– Gisela Richter, 1882 – 1972

Richter was an influential English, American, Italian archaeologist and art historian, specializing in Greek and Roman art. She never married and single status may have been what she was referring to as "the best possible result."

> **"Even a mistake may turn out to be the one thing necessary to a worthwhile achievement. ... The only real mistake is the one from which we learn nothing."**
>
> – Henry Ford, 1863 – 1947

Henry Ford was founder of the Ford Motor Company and developed the assembly line technique of mass production. His introduction of the Ford Model T revolutionized transportation in America. Ford made many mistakes. A big one was a book titled, *The International Jew; The World's Foremost Problem*, which was translated into a number of European languages and published in Germany in 1924. In July 1938, after Germany annexed Austria, Ford accepted the Grand Cross of the Order of the German Eagle. He blamed Jews for provoking pogroms and starting both World Wars. But when shown photos of concentration camp atrocities, Ford apparently learned something, far too late.

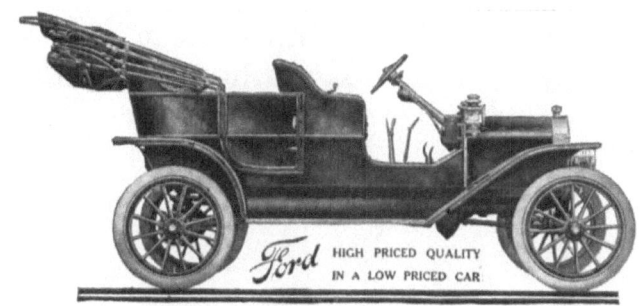

"The way to accelerate your success is to double your failure rate."

– Thomas J. Watson, 1854 – 1934

See earlier entry about Thomas Watson. If doubling one's failure rate is the key to success, there must be a lot of successful people in this world.

"I don't know the key to success, but the key to failure is trying to please everybody."

– Bill Cosby

Cosby is an American stand-up comedian and actor once known as "America's Dad" for the lovable character he played on *The Cosby Show*, the number one TV show in America from 1985 to 1989. Since 1965, Cosby started being dogged by accusations of sexual abuse that he managed to settle with many of his accusers until, starting in 2000, multiple accusers began to go public. He was found guilty and sentenced to prison in 2018. Though the conviction was overturned by the Pennsylvania Supreme Court in 2021, further civil suits against him continue. He failed. Perhaps – only in his mind – he was trying to please.

Bob Seeman

Persistence in error

"Any man can make mistakes, but only an idiot persists in his error."

– Marcus Tullius Cicero, 106 BCE – 43 BCE

Cicero was an accomplished Roman orator, a lawyer, a statesman, philosopher, and a sceptic. He was against dictatorship and spoke out repeatedly against Mark Antony. This persistent error resulted in his assassination. According to historians, the Renaissance was first and foremost a revival of Cicero's writings and, through them, a revival of the Classics. Global culture owes much to Cicero.

> ***"The definition of insanity is doing the same thing over and over again and expecting a different result."***
>
> – Albert Einstein, 1879 – 1955 (attributed)

Though this quotation has been erroneously attributed to Einstein, it has also seen attributions to Mark Twain and Benjamin Franklin and many other deep thinkers. A more likely source is the 12 step program of Alcoholics Anonymous. That context makes much more sense than attributing the quotation to a scientist because scientists are always repeating and re-repeating their experiments. That's what they do.

"I got myself into this, and I'll get myself even deeper into this."

– Anonymous

Just as Zig Ziglar explained in the description to his quotation above, this anonymous person thinks that denial is a river in Egypt.

> *"If we don't see a failure as a challenge to modify our approach, but rather as a problem with ourselves, as a personality defect, we will immediately feel overwhelmed."*
>
> – Anthony Robbins

Tony Robbins is a motivational speaker who has inspired a lot of people to get going. This has not kept him free of a number of legal issues and controversies (copyright infringement, rule violation, sexual harassment accusations). These may or may not result from personality defects.

"Good judgment comes from experience, and experience comes from bad judgment."

– Rita Mae Brown

Rita Mae Brown is an American feminist writer. She has written a large number of novels and murder mysteries. The experience she refers to may be from her engagement in feminist struggles and the divisive factions within the movement.

> *"I never made a mistake in my life. I thought I did once, but I was wrong."*
>
> – Charles M. Schulz, 1922 – 2000

Schulz was the cartoonist who created the comic strip *Peanuts*, featuring Charlie Brown and Snoopy. It has been said, "Peanuts pretty much defines the modern comic strip." At one time, *Peanuts* was featured daily in 2,600 papers in 75 countries, in 21 languages. Cartoonists throughout the United States honored Schulz on Nov. 26, 2022, on what would have been his 100th birthday for making few, if any, mistakes.

Power in Mistake

Bob Seeman

Excuses

"We made too many wrong mistakes."

– Yogi Berra, 1925 – 2015

Berra was a Yankees Major Baseball League's Hall of Famer. This quotation refers to the Yankees losing the 1960 world series to the Pittsburgh Pirates, but it can be applied to many life situations.

"In politics, as in grammar, the mistake that everyone makes is declared the rule."

– André Malraux, 1901 – 1976

Malraux was a French novelist who won the prestigious Prix Goncourt in 1933. After the War, when de Gaulle was President, Malraux became France's minister of cultural affairs with a mission to bring culture to everyone. He was widely recognized for his attempts to make this a reality and, for this reason, his ashes were moved to the Panthéon in Paris in 1996, on the 20th anniversary of his death. His quotation is accurate. When grammar rules are repeatedly broken, the error becomes the standard. In politics, too, when rules are repeatedly broken, the transgression becomes tradition.

"If all else fails, immortality can always be assured by spectacular error."

– John Kenneth Galbraith, 1908 – 2006

Galbraith was a Canadian-American economist who taught at Harvard University and wrote bestselling texts on post-Keynesian economics. He also wrote novels. Other economists considered him something of an iconoclast because he didn't use mathematical modeling and was of the opinion that economic rules changed according to one's cultural milieu. He has received a lot of criticism, which, according to his quotation, should help make his legacy immortal.

"They've finally come up with the perfect office computer. If it makes a mistake, it blames another computer."

– Milton Berle, 1908 – 2002

Berle was an American actor and comedian. He was a very funny man, often helped by planting his mother, Sadie, in the audience to whip up laughter when he made his entrance. He would then say, "Lady, you've got all night to make a fool of yourself. I've only got an hour!" Other one liners: "A committee is a group that keeps minutes and loses hours." "A good wife always forgives a husband when she's wrong."

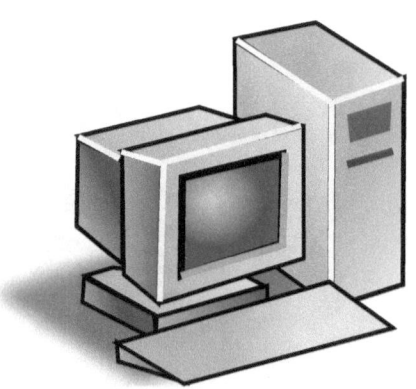

> ## *"The greatest mistake we make is living in constant fear that we will make one."*
>
> – John C. Maxwell

John Maxwell is an American evangelical Christian pastor, author, and speaker. His books, most of which are about the qualities that make for leadership, have sold millions of copies. Because people are afraid to make mistakes, they rush to buy Maxwell's books so that they learn how not to make them.

Coverups

> *"I covered the Vietnam War. I remember the lies that were told, the lives that were lost – and the shock when, twenty years after the war ended, former Defense Secretary Robert S. McNamara admitted he knew it was a mistake all along."*
>
> – Walter Cronkite, 1916 – 2009

Walter Cronkite was an American broadcast journalist known for anchoring the CBS Evening News (1962–1981). And ending each broadcast with "And that's the way it is." Cronkite visited Vietnam in 1968. In his Vietnam report, he said: "…it is increasingly clear to this reporter that the only rational way out… will be to negotiate, not as victors, but as an honorable people who… did the best they could." This may have influenced Presidents Johnson and Nixon to end the war.

> "Nixon's grand mistake was his failure to understand that Americans are forgiving, and if he had admitted error early and apologized to the country, he would have escaped."
>
> – Bob Woodward

Bob Woodward is an American investigative journalist who became famous when, with Carl Bernstein, he reported on the Watergate scandal. He has written or co-written over 20 books on the ins and outs of American politics. Admitting error is good advice but hard advice for most people to take.

"To make a mistake is human, but to blame it on someone else, that's even more human."
– Anonymous

Anonymous is a good psychologist.

"I am being frank about myself in this book. I tell of my first mistake on page 850."

– Henry Kissinger

Henry Kissinger and his family fled Germany in 1938 and were admitted to the U.S. . Kissinger was 15 so never lost his accent. He served as Secretary of State and National Security Advisor under Presidents Nixon and Ford. Because he negotiated a ceasefire between the US and the Vietcong in Vietnam, he received a 1973 Nobel Peace Prize. Kissinger also pioneered the détente with Russia and the opening of US relations with China. Like everyone, he made mistakes, and is often accused of not speaking out against war crimes committed by America's allies.

Bob Seeman

Forgiveness

> **"If an apology is followed by an excuse or a reason, it means they are going to commit same mistake again they just apologized for."**
>
> – Amit Kalantri

Amit Kalantri is an Indian magician and mentalist. He says that he can read people's minds. So he can tell which people will repeat their mistakes. This is a handy skill to have.

"Love truth, but pardon error."
– Voltaire, 1694 – 1778

Voltaire, a nom de plume, was a prolific French writer and philosopher. Probably his most famous work is *Candide ou l'Optimisme*, published in 1759. Voltaire was an outspoken advocate of civil liberties and recognized that those who are truly free to speak their mind often make mistakes. That's par for the course. But those who follow orders not because they agree but because they have no choice, that is the biggest mistake.

Bob Seeman

Life lessons

> *"Mistakes are a part of being human. Precious life lessons that can only be learned the hard way. Unless it's a fatal mistake, which, at least, others can learn from."*
>
> – Al Franken

Franken is a comedian and a former U.S. Senator. He was accused of sexual abuse of women during photo ops, which he said were intended as jokes. He offered to speak to the Senate Ethics Committee to explain his side of the story but Senate Minority Leader Chuck Schumer insisted he resign. Two mistakes were made – Schumer's for demanding the resignation, and Franken's for hastily conceding.

"Never mistake motion for action."

– Ernest Hemingway, 1899 – 1981

Hemingway was an American novelist and short story writer noted for his iceberg or omission theory of good writing. It was a minimalist style that focused on surface events without suggesting underlying themes or hidden emotions. He was very economical with his language, as can also be seen in this quotation. If expanded, the quotation would say that actions are meaningful; they are more than just motion. Don't make the mistake of equating the two. He would have said that his final act, deliberately shooting himself in the head, was an action.

"If I had to live my life again, I'd make the same mistakes, only sooner."

– Tallulah Bankhead, 1903 – 1968

Tallulah Bankhead was an American movie actress. She apparently spoke openly about her vices (liberal causes, cigarettes, alcohol, drugs, serial relationships with men and women) and, as her quotation shows, did not regret them. Another of her quotations: "I'm as pure as the driven slush." She was, in her own words, someone "who lived for the moment." When asked about her sexual preferences, Tallulah said she was "ambisextrous."

"Freedom is not worth having if it does not include the freedom to make mistakes."

– Mahatma Gandhi, 1869 – 1948

Mohandas Gandhi, known as Mahatma (a person regarded with reverence), a lawyer and anti-colonial nationalist, used non-violent resistance to mount a successful campaign for India's independence from Britain. He hoped for an independent India based on religious pluralism. His mistake was to underestimate the irresolvable nature of conflicts between Hindus and Muslims.

"Live as if you were living for the second time and as if you had made a lot of mistakes the first time."

– Viktor Frankl, 1905 – 1997

Frankl, an Austrian neuropsychiatrist, was an extraordinary man, the founder of a school of psychotherapy called logotherapy, a form of existential therapy, which he describes in his autobiographical book, *Man's Search for Meaning*. He had a chance to live a second time after surviving Nazi concentration camps.

> *"Many a man in love with a dimple makes the mistake of marrying the whole girl."*
> – Stephen Leacock, 1869 – 1944

Stephen Leacock was a Canadian humorist. He taught at the elite Toronto school, Upper Canada College, his own alma mater. His essays and short stories became mandatory reading in Canadian schools. Some were turned into films. What he's saying here is that it's a mistake to think that all that glitters is gold.

"No one is listening until you make a mistake."

– Anonymous

Anonymous always gets it right. All your on-the-button pithy comments go unnoticed but make a blooper, and everyone's listening.

> *"I had the vocation for politics. What I didn't have was any aptitude for political combat. I took the attacks personally, which is a great mistake. It's never personal: It's just business. It was ever thus."*
>
> – Michael Ignatieff

Ignatieff is a Canadian academic and former politician who served as the leader of the Liberal Party of Canada from 2008 until 2011. In the 2011 federal election, Ignatieff lost his own seat and the Liberal Party had its worst showing in the entirety of its history. Ignatieff resigned. Sometimes vocation is not enough.

"When a doctor makes a mistake, it's best to bury the subject."

– Woody Allen

Woody Allen is a well known American film director and comedian. He began writing jokes for established comedians when he was 15. Making jokes about death can, for some, be a good coping mechanism to deal with the fear of death. Woody Allen characters are obsessed with death.

"The greater the funding, the longer it takes to make the mistake."

– Anonymous

Anonymous is onto something here. If you're well-funded, it takes longer for mistakes to become apparent.

"God don't make no mistakes... that's how He got to be God."

– Carroll O'Connor, 1924 – 2001

O'Connor played Archie Bunker, in the TV show, *All in the Family*, the role for which he won four Emmy Awards. Archie Bunker said many funny things on the show and he might have said this: "but if He made no mistakes, how come He keeps changing things?"

"Live rich, die poor; never make the mistake of doing it the other way round."

– Walter Annenberg, 1908 – 2002

Annenberg was an American businessman and philanthropist who owned several newspapers and magazines and was, for 5 years, US ambassador to the United Kingdom. Only the very rich could say "Live rich, die poor". Both rich and poor get it wrong: "The man with a toothache thinks everyone happy whose teeth are sound. The poverty-stricken man makes the same mistake about the rich man."

> *"A life spent making mistakes is not only more honourable but more useful than a life spent doing nothing."*
>
> – George Bernard Shaw, 1856 – 1950

George Bernard Shaw's humorous quotations have already been demonstrated earlier. He held many contentious views but was always able to express them in witty ways.

"Never interrupt your enemy when he is making a mistake."

– Napoleon Bonaparte, 1769 – 1821

History considers Napoleon Bonaparte a great military man and a great French emperor. The Russians must have heard of this advice before Napoleon invaded Russia because they didn't interrupt him. They avoided engagement and instead retreated. They waited him out until he realized on his own that he had made a great mistake. Napoleon lost 360,000 men in this mistaken invasion.

> **"Nowadays most people die of a sort of creeping common sense, and discover when it is too late that the only things one never regrets are one's mistakes."**
>
> – Oscar Wilde, 1854 – 1900

It is good to know that Oscar Wilde (quoted earlier as well) did not regret his mistakes.

> **"Remember that life's greatest lessons are usually learned at the worst times and from the worst mistakes."**
>
> – Anonymous

If a person is into learning, then it's imperative to live in terrible times and to make terrible mistakes.

> ## *"How would you like a job where, when you made a mistake, a big red light goes on and 18,000 people boo?"*
> – Jacques Plante, 1929 – 1986

Plante was a Canadian ice hockey goaltender with the Montreal Canadiens, the Toronto Maple Leafs, and the Boston Bruins. He was considered an important hockey innovator, the first, for example, to skate behind the net to stop the puck. He was also famous for his fibreglass mask. As he says, private mistakes are okay but hard to bear when exposed to the world.

> **"There are worse things than getting a call for a wrong number at 4 am. It could be a right number."**
>
> – Doug Larson, 1926 – 2017

Larson wrote a daily column called "Doug's Dugout" for a Wisconsin newspaper. He was described as the master of zany one-liners. Another example, "To err is human; to admit it, superhuman."

"I changed my password to 'incorrect', so anytime I forget and enter the wrong thing, the computer tells me what it is."

"My son came home and said 'I got a D in my maths'. I said, 'That's really bad' and my wife said, 'you need to stop doing his homework.'"

Power in Mistake

Bob Seeman

Acknowledgments

I would like to acknowledge and thank all those who assisted me with this book.

www.ingramcontent.com/pod-product-compliance
Lightning Source LLC
Chambersburg PA
CBHW031928240526
45464CB00023B/2210